Joe Battaglia articulates v ... our cultural divide in ord ...
America Good Again identifies the intentional social reengineering and unintentional ignorance that have brought us to the place of fear, anger, and hopelessness today. Understanding the past allows us to enter intellectually honest dialogue to discover solutions and change our future. This small but great book is one I can easily endorse for its journalistic excellence and compassionate appeal to help us break free from deception and live united in life-giving truth, according to God's design, plan, and purpose.

PAMELA CHRISTIAN, DD; ORDAINED INTERNATIONAL
MINISTER; AWARD-WINNING AUTHOR; KEYNOTE SPEAKER;
MEDIA HOST, HOLY SPIRIT BROADCAST NETWORK

In this riveting new book, Joe Battaglia's clarifying, Christ-centered wisdom and common sense deliver a message America desperately needs: we'll truly become great again when we stop screaming at each other long enough to find common ground. Boy, do we ever need this important message on healing our national discourse!

MIKE GALLAGHER, SALEM RADIO NETWORK,
NEW YORK, NEW YORK

Joe Battaglia marshals his considerable life experience as a journalist/broadcaster, author, and para-church expert in *Make America Good Again* to offer insight and bridge the great chasm that has opened up in American life—one that divides us not only in politics but also in the church and among families. Want to learn how to talk about gun control, climate change, and poverty in a manner befitting a self-proclaimed follower of Christ? Then buy this book! In fact, get two copies: one for yourself and one for anyone with whom you feel a sundered relationship because of all things political.

HUGH HEWITT, *NEW YORK TIMES* BEST-SELLING AUTHOR; WASHINGTON POST COLUMNIST; SALEM RADIO NETWORK HOST

The ever-ingenious Joseph Battaglia once again gets us to pause, reflect, and think deeper about our current cultural mess and the chaos that has plagued too many of our hearts, minds, parties, institutions, and souls. This must-read book offers a convicting exploration of all we are called to: humility, truth, mercy, and love. You'll be better off for reading Battaglia's latest work.

BILLY HALLOWELL, DIRECTOR OF COMMUNICATIONS AND CONTENT, PUREFLIX.COM; AUTHOR, *THE ARMAGEDDON CODE*, *FAULT LINE*, AND *LEFT STANDING*

My friend, Joe Battaglia, reminds us of Alexis de Tocqueville's big idea: goodness must be at the heart of America. *Make America Good Again* is timely, welcome, and important. The freedom we have enjoyed in America these last two and a half centuries can only continue if we understand this idea, pass it on, and live it out.

ERIC METAXAS, *NEW YORK TIMES* BEST-SELLING AUTHOR; HOST OF THE NATIONALLY SYNDICATED *ERIC METAXAS RADIO SHOW*

In a thoroughly thoughtful, provocative, and urgent sense, Joe Battaglia takes on some of today's sacred cows but does so in a winsome way. Whether you agree with him or not, you will be a better person because he has forced you to evaluate the issues of today.

KEVIN MCCULLOUGH, FOX NEWS COMMENTATOR; HOST OF THE NATIONALLY SYNDICATED *THE KEVIN MCCULLOUGH SHOW*

If there was ever a book for this precarious and uncertain time, it is *Make America Good Again*! Joe Battaglia applies his unique combination of wisdom, wit, and insight to address some of the greatest challenges of our time.

JEANNE ZAINO, PH.D.; PROFESSOR OF POLITICAL SCIENCE AND INTERNATIONAL STUDIES, IONA COLLEGE; SENIOR ADVISOR, APPLIEDTECHONOMICS, PUBLIC SECTOR

MAKE

12.5 Biblical Principles

AMERICA

to Unite Our Nation,

GOOD

Restore True Greatness,

AGAIN

and Reshape Our Political Rhetoric

JOE BATTAGLIA

FOREWORD BY **TODD STARNES**
host of *The Todd Starnes Radio Show*

BroadStreet
Ⓟ Ⓤ Ⓑ Ⓛ Ⓘ Ⓢ Ⓗ Ⓘ Ⓝ Ⓖ

BroadStreet Publishing Group®, LLC
Savage, Minnesota, USA
www.broadstreetpublishing.com

MAKE AMERICA GOOD AGAIN: 12.5 Biblical
Principles to Unite Our Nation, Restore True Greatness, and
Reshape Our Political Rhetoric

978-1-4245-6170-4 (paperback)
978-1-4245-6171-1 (e-book)

Stock or custom editions of BroadStreet Publishing titles
may be purchased in bulk for educational, business, ministry,
fundraising, or sales promotional use. For information, please
email info@broadstreetpublishing.com.

Cover and interior by Garborg Design at GarborgDesign.com

Printed in The United States of America
20 21 22 23 24 5 4 3 2 1

To my daughter, Alanna,
who always inspires me
toward goodness and continually
challenges me to that end!

Further, I pray that our nation's children
will see civility and good heartedness
return to our land.

Contents

FOREWORD

Goodness is all about how we resist in bowing to the god of self-aggrandizement to pursue true humility, speak truth, show mercy, love the unlovable, and even embrace opposition. To be just as comfortable with the immigrant, the oppressed, the voiceless, and the powerless as with those from Silicon Valley and Wall Street. To identify with the dreams and aspirations of those living in either red or blue states.

But how do we rise above the din of the plethora of demeaning voices shouting at us every day during an election year filled with ugly, demeaning, embarrassing, and hateful rhetoric with disingenuous rants from both sides? It will undoubtedly remain that way unless we change the narrative, which is neither right nor left.

I've been reporting from the front lines of political wars for more than a decade, and to be perfectly honest with you, it's gotten a little noisy. Okay, it's gotten really noisy, and more often than not, the discourse has turned coarse.

That's why Joe Battaglia's new book is so important for the national conversation. He's the son of an immigrant who cuts through the noise of the day to remind us that our differences should unite us, not divide us. Joe's book shows us the path we must take in order to make America good again.

Todd Starnes

INTRODUCTION

Alexis de Tocqueville was the French political thinker and historian best known for his *Democracy in America* (appearing in two volumes: 1835 and 1840), which was published after his travels in the United States. It's considered an early work of political science, and in it, he astutely captures the essence of the Great Experiment that was America's. His observations about what made us a truly great nation are illuminating.

The following quote is often attributed to him but is not actually found in his two-volume set. That said, in tone and content, it certainly could have been said by him! Regardless, it speaks volumes about what has made America great:

> I sought for the greatness and
> genius of America in her commodious

harbors and her ample rivers—and it was not there . . . in her fertile fields and boundless forests and it was not there . . . in her rich mines and her vast world commerce—and it was not there . . . in her democratic Congress and her matchless Constitution—and it was not there. Not until I went into the churches of America and heard her pulpits aflame with righteousness did I understand the secret of her genius and power. America is great because she is good, and if America ever ceases to be good, she will cease to be great.

De Toqueville may not have said this, but he did visit houses of worship and comment on the pivotal role that faith in God played in establishing the mindset of freedom and goodness that separated America from all other nations, as captured in this quote of his: "Liberty cannot be established without morality, nor morality without faith." He understood the clear, symbiotic relationship between liberty and faith in God.

> Liberty cannot be established without morality, nor morality without faith.

Scripture says that "righteousness exalts a nation" (Proverbs 14:34 NIV). What great truths were expounded from those "pulpits aflame with righteousness" that made America good? We'll explore that as we suggest alternative perspectives on key party platforms and hot-button issues framed within biblical principles. It may even help us draw a roadmap that leads us back to being good again.

Section One

Foundations and Party Platforms

Chapter 1

DIFFERENCES MAKE US STRONGER

Inscribed on the back of every coin are the Latin words *E pluribus unum*. That may be all someone ever sees of Latin nowadays. I suspect that most Americans know the phrase means "one from many." The heterogeneous makeup of our population has long represented our nation's genius in that we are one nation formed from many different people. Simply, we are all different yet one. Not that we are all the same and one.

There is a reason why this simple Latin phrase embodies America's greatness, regardless of the historical revisionists, who would rewrite much about our history simply because they are either ignorant of facts or prefer to overlay their modern-day perspectives on anything that happened many years ago that does not fit their current politically correct agendas.

The wonder of the "one from many" motto was instilled in me very early in my life as the son of immigrants. My parents were born in Italy, immigrated to America in the 1930s, and never went back. My paternal grandparents lived with us as well, reinforcing the appreciation of my roots *and* their perspectives of the privilege of being an American. We never held those two sentiments in tension in my family. They are the two sides of the coin that represent the strength of our nation. Unfortunately, much of our current national narrative seems to have forgotten that our strength lies in our differences—and our ability to see beyond differences for the greater good.

My father was not quite seventeen when he came to America. As such, he had vivid memories of his childhood and young adulthood in Italy, living in a small mountain town in Calabria in clear sight of the sea about eight miles down the mountain. He would tell me about his idyllic life as a child, especially during the summer months, when he and his friends would walk down the mountain and spend several days at the beach without coming home. He'd take some salami and cheese from the cellar, catch fish in the sea, and sleep under the stars on the beach. His family was self-sufficient because they grew or raised everything they needed. It was their version of Mayberry. It sounded so good.

But then he would tell me stories of how hard it was in the winter when he got here to America, especially working during the Great

Depression. How he had to go without a coat one winter because he could not afford one, and how my grandfather would get up at four o'clock in the morning to walk five miles to a neighboring town to get to work at six. I asked why he didn't take a bus. His answer was simple: they always walked in Italy, and it was easier on flat land with sidewalks than in the mountains. Plus, you saved the five cents it cost for the bus ride and bought some food with that nickel. Oh.

I asked him one day, "Why even come to America and face the hardships of living in a foreign environment—start all over, work into the evening, and all the other things that accompany an immigrant's new life in a new land?"

And again, his answer was simple. First, they could sense that war was coming in Europe. Plus America was the land of opportunity. It afforded a person through hard work what luxury and ease couldn't: identity and self-realization. You see, there is something within the heart of each of us that yearns to realize what we are wired to be and do—and then to be free to do it.

That heartfelt yearning is exemplified best in these stirring lines of the Declaration of Independence: "We hold these truths to be self-evident, that all men are created equal, that they are endowed by their Creator with certain unalienable Rights, that among these are Life, Liberty and the pursuit of Happiness."[1]

The Great Experiment in establishing a new nation was based upon the understanding that since "all men are created equal" and in God's image, people can coexist *if* they remain glued to that fact. The Founding Fathers understood that in order for the universe to work in sync with the Creator, they must naturally observe this foundational principle.

---

1   "Declaration of Independence: A Transcription," *National Archives*, https://www.archives.gov/founding-docs/declaration-transcript. Historically, the term *men* has been used generically to denote both men and women. Contrary to politically correct propaganda, diversity did not start with political correctness.

Inherent to our national motto is an understanding of the greatness of plurality and the necessity of having people who are different from each other speak into each other's lives. We can only act upon this if indeed we believe that God made us in his image, and we are therefore equal. Every one of us. The Founding Fathers established America upon the realization that we *must* have differences to be more fully one. The diversity exhibited in creation is clear evidence of this universal principle. No two snowflakes are alike. Identical twins are not even identical. God's creation is manifest in such a way that differences actually create similarities. Or they should.

> God made us in his image, and we are therefore equal. Every one of us.

Part of the issue we face today is the lack of appreciation of our differences. It's easy to hide within so-called communities of sameness online.

We create straw men out of people who think, act, or look differently from us and blame them for the ills in our world. But the reality is that we all cannot believe the same way or even the same things. Sameness and similarity do not enhance people's ability to come together; instead, differences can contribute to establishing oneness as they fill in the gaps left by sameness. When differences come together in an appreciation of people's God-given opportunities, the outcome is strength, not weakness. Just the opposite of what many seem to think.

Those who only want to be with their own must be the loneliest people around. In the end, we are the ones who suffer from the ills of sameness. When we lose sight of that, intolerance grows. It's no wonder that the prevailing mindset today is *us-versus-them*, which we see played out so dramatically in our culture, especially in the political arena. This mentality is so disastrous to oneness because it prevents true intersection in life.

We get along best when we interact and rely

on each other for our sustenance. I am much more likely to get to know you, appreciate you, and even befriend you when I'm sweating alongside you for a common goal. I may even learn from you and appreciate things I would never be confronted with unless I heard your voice, listened to what you said, and sensed the hope in your soul, which sounds a lot like my heart and soul. You can't get that opportunity in an online community or in believing like everyone else. It's the way the universe operates. There is no adequate substitute for looking into your eyes to see the eternity in your soul and to hear the heartbeat of your dream.

So it brings us back to my father's idyllic life in that small, nondescript Italian mountainside town. Why leave Shangri-La for potential hardship, sweat, and uncomfortable surroundings? Why leave behind one's family to live among strangers? Simple. It's the way we're wired and what makes the human family spin. Community fulfills the longing in our hearts and souls for differences that will complete us. Not the same things that only make us stale. And boring.

Resist the political rhetoric from both sides of the aisle and the mistaken notion that you'll find security in being with people just like you. You aren't really safe. Get in the game, be with others unlike you, and find out what you were truly meant to be and do.

America will become good again when it understands that we only find that in the community of "one from many."

Chapter 2

THERE'S NO
US *vs*. THEM.
IT'S JUST US.

If we understand that our differences make us stronger, then what is in our national psyche that has created such divisiveness among people with differing opinions? Why are we more suspicious of each other than ever?

Our nation was founded on a belief system

whose foundation is the universal respect for all individuals since God created all in his image. There is a moral code beyond us that establishes that foundation, and if you trifle with that and eliminate the notion of God, then the respect for life diminishes as well. Unfortunately, that very foundation which enhances tolerance and understanding is being systematically deleted from our public square, mainly in the name of political correctness.

First, it might be helpful to provide some background information on political correctness. And don't just take my word for it. Check this out for yourself. Most people are not aware of the Marxist roots of political correctness that started in Europe in the 1920s as a subtle way to redefine language and symbols of culture in Marxist terms.

Initially, the idea was to pit the working class against the ruling class, which did not take very much effort back in the early twentieth century, given the conditions in Europe after the First

World War. This new ideology took hold in Europe and was eventually exported to America.

Under the guise of equality and tolerance, the true intent of the PC movement was to create an *us-versus-them* mentality by pitting people against each other—rich against poor, male against female, victims against their oppressors. The idea was to create artificial rifts and paranoia between groups.

The PC goal was and is to identify certain minority groups (not necessarily ethnic, but the poor and oppressed at first) who would be the good guys, because they were kept at bay by the ruling classes (the bad guys), which were primarily white and wealthy in Europe. Since many of the proponents of this new ideology were atheists, who viewed religion as a tool of the wealthy, ruling class, they had to include religion, particularly Christianity, as another one of the antagonists in the class struggle. They particularly singled out Judeo-Christian thought for deconstruction because its symbols and theology were so antithetical to Marxist thinking and the prevailing anti-Semitism of the day. Of course, we all know where Marxist thinking took us in the twentieth century . . . to Stalinist Russia, communist China, and the killing fields of the Khmer Rouge of Cambodia.

Eventually, that ideology came to America, where the fertile ground of the 1960s radical counterculture provided the right conditions to fuel the growth of the PC movement. Political correctness needs good guys and bad guys to pit against each other, and in this environment, there were ready-made antagonists and protagonists—the necessary ingredients to a good Marxist revolution. And the establishment of a politically correct movement was born.

But political correctness was not new. In the New Testament, Jesus steps into a similar politically correct environment of his day and proclaims something entirely radical: the state is not our enemy. And neither is the ruling class, the wealthy, the poor, white males, etc. He obliterates the *us-versus-them* mentality that is at the core of the politically correct agenda that was so rampant in his society then and is in our society today.

He says now what he said two thousand years ago: render to Caesar what belongs to Caesar and to God what belongs to God. He wants us to go beyond the cultural rivalry fostered by political correctness and simply be lights to truth. He then boldly proclaims that God is bigger than the state, which exists only by God's grace and design. It has limited power. It cannot rule over the longing of the human spirit that cries out for freedom.

Did you ever wonder where the idea behind "Life, Liberty and the pursuit of Happiness" came from? Not from *The Communist Manifesto*. Its roots were in the First Great Awakening in the mid-1700s that stirred people's hearts to the concept of a biblical freedom of self-determination as a child of God, not as a ward of the state with its imposed caste systems, which were prevalent throughout the world. A religious revival set the precedent for the foundation of the American Revolution that de Tocqueville recognized as the quality that made our nation great.

> Let's celebrate our differences openly and civilly to dispel the notion that "us versus them" is part of our national narrative.

Let's celebrate our differences openly and civilly to dispel the notion that "us versus them" is part of our national narrative. Jesus as a model demands honesty in the way we interact with each other. His way fosters freedom and despises intolerance. But he also demands an ethic beyond our ability to live it and gives us boundaries for our safety. Such an ethic also tells a government that it exists for the people not for itself. And, to the chagrin of many, it tells us that we are not gods.

See political correctness for what it is: intellectual dishonesty with a divisive spirit. Don't engage in the us-versus-them discussion. America will become good again when we realize it's always been just *us*.

Chapter 3

Find Common Ground Despite Our Differences

Have you ever heard the adage that you should never discuss religion and politics in certain social circumstances? Well a few years ago, it was both politics and religion that resulted in an invitation for me to go to Washington, DC, to meet with some leaders of a particular political party and one of their think tanks.

The events leading up to that invitation were pretty interesting. In 2004 I had been involved in a campaign called *Redeem the Vote,* which encouraged young people of faith to register to vote. The campaign was rather successful in its effort to convince young men and women to download voter registration forms. It also garnered lots of national press for its chief spokesperson and founder, as well as for some artists I had enlisted to help voice a number of public service announcements that I had written, produced, and cleared on radio stations nationwide.

We had so much success in that endeavor that we (the founder and I) were invited to meet with some leaders of this particular party because they said we were the only non-strident evangelicals they knew. That was a sad indictment—either of the evangelicals they had met or of themselves for never taking the time to associate with evangelicals. Or maybe it was a little bit of both. However, isn't it like most of us, who rarely hang out with people whose worldviews are dramatically different from our own?

If we're Christ-followers, Jesus prefers that we choose to be around those who are different from us. Isolating ourselves only with those with whom we agree on everything is the opposite of how Jesus interacted and intersected with people unlike him, the social outcasts of his day, like the Samaritan woman at the well (John 4) or prostitutes or lepers. The social calendars of many people during that period were pretty predetermined.

In our case, the people we met in DC rarely intersected with Christ-followers. If two groups are busy going in opposite political and cultural directions, they rarely take the time to consider that there may be some reason to intersect with each other. Either group might consider the other as the leper of their world, which is sad. Our interaction in DC resulted in wonderful new friendships between several of those individuals whose lives would have been untouched by mine, and vice versa, had we not decided to go outside of ourselves to find each other.

During one of our meetings in a rather nice home in Georgetown, we answered questions about how best to work with evangelicals on issues that supposedly divided us, such as abortion, immigration, gay rights, etc.

At one point, one individual asked me, "What is the evangelical middle ground on abortion?"

"There really is none," I replied. "One cannot have a middle ground on the sanctity-of-life issue as it's firmly grounded in an inviolate law of God about when life begins and who can determine a disturbance in its continuum."

At that point, the man threw his arms in the air. "See, there's no talking with you evangelicals because you refuse to discuss things like this!"

I replied kindly that he was asking me the wrong question. "It's not about finding the middle ground to when life begins and when it's okay to summarily take that life," I told him. "The better question would be how to find common ground, not middle ground." I took a breath and went on. "Middle ground suggests that we compromise on something we have no right in doing—violating our conscience and our understanding of God's Word. That's not finding middle ground; that's a sellout. Or intellectual dishonesty at best."

I continued to say that the better way is trying to find common ground so that even if we may not agree on a particular issue, we can still strive to find what we can agree on that satisfies both of our positions. "Can we honestly work to both minimize the opportunity for abortion and still protect someone's right under the Constitution?" I asked him. "And still respect each other's positions while maintaining a civil discourse with each other?"

I suggested, "So, as good management strategy would dictate, we should start at our desired goal. In this case, the obvious common ground is to reduce the number of abortions as much as possible, if not entirely. Most evangelicals would rather see fewer abortions each year than seeing no reduction year in and year out. A platform of attrition is one way to address the issue and would allow for pro-life people from either party to speak to the issue and forge a model that can work."

He looked surprised and intrigued. As a result of that evening's very interesting interaction, they retained me to help craft some understanding of how evangelicals think on certain issues and what could be common ground between the two groups. We published a white paper suggesting common ground on some key social issues, thereby creating more of a dialogue between us that even allowed God to show up in the discussion.

As a Christ-follower, my work is simply to show up in scenarios that might allow his presence a place at the table. If I recuse myself from the discussions because I have an allegiance to one idea over another or one political expression over another, others will never hear my opinion. If I never enter a foreign environment emotionally and intellectually, then I will never expose others to what I believe. And if I never know what others believe, then I will never be able to better understand them.

Being a Christ-follower is all about finding common ground with everyone. Jesus did that exceptionally well. The Samaritan woman at the well in the Gospel of John is a good case in point. The powerful thing about this story is that Jesus went out of his way to find someone whom society said he should avoid or disregard. Maybe not unlike the people I met and their aversion to Christ-followers.

> Being a Christ-follower is all about finding common ground with everyone.

I realize many people run from evangelicals because they know only what we stand against, not what we stand for. Unfortunate, but often true. Like the woman at the well, I suspect my new friends feared that an association with evangelicals would be more about judgment and condemnation. They probably see more illustrations of those things than they see the Mother Teresa kind of love and forgiveness, and that may cloud their thinking. I get it.

But the Bible is clear that Jesus does not condemn, and neither should we. The most famous passage in all of Scripture may be John 3:16, which speaks of God's love for man by sending his Son to die for us. The next verse says, "For God did not send his Son into the world to condemn the world, but to save the world through him" (3:17 NIV). We see that exhibited plainly in his dealings with the woman at the well (John 4) and the woman caught in adultery (John 8). He forgave both and asked them to discontinue their lifestyle. But he didn't chide them for their sin or condemn them. He chose to intersect with their lives to show them God's love and to reorient their focus, which was clouded by the religious thinking they were accustomed to.

Jesus confronted sin in a loving manner. Conviction brings love into the equation whereas condemnation leaves no room for love. Conviction is born of love, condemnation from a lack of compassion. Some of God's so-called representatives are too quick to condemn because they misunderstand God's love and their role in the kingdom. Handling absolute truth can be difficult. It can make some people hard, unloving, and unable to find common ground. Isaiah 1:18 says, "'Come now, let us reason together,' says the Lord" (ESV). Unreasonable people, whether right or wrong, hardly ever make headway on tough issues. For others, confronting tough issues illumines our weaknesses and drives us to find common ground with others, sometimes through tears.

My good friend Dr. Steve Brown says that righteousness without tears is arrogance. I'm afraid the world has seen too much of our righteousness and too little of our tears. I'll bet Jesus spoke with compassion to both the woman at the well and the woman caught in adultery. His eyes may even have gotten moist when he understood their situation.

So my time in DC with my newfound friends once again showed me that my role is to find a way to help all people find that common ground between themselves and God. People who may be very different from me politically are really much the same as me in so many other ways. It just takes some time to look for the commonality between us. That's called *communication*. And when communication happens, our role as defined in 2 Corinthians 5:18–20 will jump out at us: we are to reestablish friendship between others and God and act as his ambassadors. That requires us to find common ground.

America will become good again when we resist the trench warfare so prevalent in our society today among people with differing opinions and among our political leaders.

Chapter 4

Tolerance

When I was a kid, I'd often sit with my father watching the old TV series *The Untouchables*. It starred Robert Stack as Elliott Ness, the leader of a group of FBI G-men who fought organized crime. Seemed like most of the bad guys had names similar to mine in that they all ended in a vowel, and they spoke the same language as my family. I'm a first-generation Italian American (both my parents were born in Italy). My paternal grandparents lived with us as well. So we were *very* Italian, complete with a chicken coop my grandfather built, the wine cellar, and the all-day family feasts that regular people called Sunday lunch.

Anyway, a particular episode of *The Untouchables* introduced yet another criminal to the story line with an Italian surname. My father loudly proclaimed his displeasure as to why everyone had to be of Italian origin, to which I replied, "Dad, probably because they were."

Today's bad guys come in a different form. If you're looking for extremists or terrorists, they can be of any nationality. It's now more about ideology than ethnicity, which makes it even more dangerous. When law enforcement authorities infiltrate extremist and illegal groups of any kind, whether they be extreme Islamic in light of 9/11, organized crime (Mafia), or white collar, there's always an outcry of profiling, and then people throw around the word *intolerant*.

In light of 9/11 and other acts of terrorism advocated by spokespersons of radical Islam, government surveillance of these groups has increased. Movies and TV shows, like *24*, centered on terrorist activity plots are replete with Islamic individuals. When the FBI targeted all the Mafia family bosses for surveillance, they didn't wiretap local hangouts of the Daughters of the American Revolution. I suspect some of you may not be familiar with this unique sorority of flag waving, apple-pie descendants of those who fought in the Revolutionary War and who could not be further from the stereotypical Mafiosi persona. Today, the politically correct police are like my father, who felt offended because people were simply stating the obvious: most of the organized crime bosses were Italian. Their names were not made up. There was no plot to defame those of Italian heritage.

An unfortunate result of the malevolent behavior of those from various ethnic backgrounds can often lead to stereotypes. And those stereotypes lead to other unfortunate incidents, often at the expense of the innocent. But in our current PC world, others tell us to stay away from offending anyone, regardless of what is obvious or even true. It seems that certain groups of people can enjoy the same endangered species status of the white tiger or humpback whale.

Society calls it tolerance to declare "no critique zones" on entire groups of people or ideologies. But is it really tolerance? For example, if you're a high-profile individual who holds a traditional view of marriage between one woman and one man and you express that belief, you may receive the wrath of activists or the media. You haven't said anything disparaging about any opposing beliefs or about anyone who may disagree with you; you have only stated what you *do* believe. Well, some people's reactions make it seem as though you'd just formed a welcoming committee for Al-Qaeda in your community.

We no longer see disagreement as an opportunity for constructive dialogue. Instead, some consider it tantamount to a hate crime. Tolerance is no longer two sides of a coin. The ones who seem to hold the politically correct power have redefined tolerance and turned it into the suppression of opinion. What good does that do? Who does that protect?

Political correctness would prefer to turn a blind eye to the obvious for fear of offending people. Most members of the Mafia are Italian, and most members of the Russian mob are, well, Russian, and most of the Islamic extremists are Muslims.

You cannot escape the obvious, and stating it could get you into trouble—just like it did with Jesus when he encountered similar situations. He would state the obvious all the time. Like when he confronted the Pharisees and said that they were like whitewashed tombs because their words sounded high and mighty, but they had no love inside of them for the people (Matthew 23:27–28). When he healed people on the Sabbath (Matthew

12:9–14), he was going against the PC status of his day. Those in power could not allow Jesus to promulgate those kinds of ideas among the people. It could be infectious.

Truth is dangerous because it is contagious. Why do you think there's so much anger and argumentative behavior among those who are trying to advance politically correct agendas? Because these agendas are not about tolerance; they're about power. And when we confront power with the obvious (truth), a spiritual reaction occurs. Today we're seeing it played out in our country and around the world.

> Truth is dangerous
> because it is contagious.

Jesus meets us in the middle of this insanity and says *he* wants to bring us peace. But to do so, he must state the obvious by confronting us with the truth—regardless of what we think about it or whether it contradicts some of the politically correct positions others admonish us to hold. When he confronted those with differing opinions and lifestyles, he did not shy away from saying what was obvious. Jesus did not tolerate sin. Neither did he condemn the person committing it. Instead, he showed them a better way: forgiveness. Jesus' dual approach of love and forgiveness enabled people to receive what they were hearing, despite the entrenchment of their sins or the blindness that gripped them.

In our PC-crazy world, some continue to rail against the obvious, hoping that enough bluster will allow them to continue in their sin or in the kinds of lifestyles that Jesus challenged. In that case, Jesus will treat them like he confronted the money changers in the temple and overturned their tables. The money changers were scamming the people coming into the temple in need of an offering for their sacrifice. He wasn't being very tolerant then. And he's not today. But wasn't he also stating the obvious?

He still chases out of us all the things we do and say that try to scam God of what's rightfully his in our lives. No amount of political will or negative press can erase the obvious facts of who Jesus is and what he claimed. He calls his followers to be north stars for the world—people of peace who exhibit true tolerance that engages everyone and draws their hearts toward their Creator. Jesus understood two thousand years ago that stating the obvious would cost something. He called his followers to speak the truth then, and he calls us to do the same today with God's grace and peace.

America will become good again when we stop screaming at each other long enough to listen. And learn.

Section Two

THE ISSUES

Chapter 5

IMMIGRATION

There has certainly been much discussion, hand-wringing, soul searching, and name calling on the issue of immigration. Aliens, immigrants, "dreamers," and refugees—however you identify them, one thing remains: everyone has a name . . . and a story. We see lots of political grandstanding on this issue by many who pick up placards to plead their causes.

As I see it, the problem is that we continue to address this issue as a political one, which may never resolve it. People will boil it down to what is legal and what is not. Or what is expedient. Or what is *fair*, which of course is impossible to measure because fairness might be the most subjective term in our lexicon. Then there are issues about security, administration, costs, humanitarian work, and the list goes on.

The more I think about the issue of immigration, the more I have come to believe that there is something that's missing from the usual water-cooler discussion. Is there a greater insight that we must realize? After we strip away the politics and semantics, we come face-to-face with basic human issues. And Scripture has ample wisdom within its pages to address most any issue that deals with the human condition.

First of all, the Bible is replete with stories of immigrants, dreamers, and refugees. From Genesis to Revelation, the grand story is really all about immigrants and aliens. Surely, we can learn something applicable for today from digging into these stories.

From the very beginning, we have drama:

- God evicted Adam and Eve from their first home, never allowing them to return. God put a "No Vacancy" sign at the entrance, and since then, no one has ever stepped foot into that environment.

- God told Abraham to emigrate from his homeland Haran to Canaan and take everything with him to start a new life. He had no idea where God was going to lead him. Sounds like a refugee to me.

- God asked Abraham's nephew Lot to leave his home and not look back because it had become so wicked.

- Jacob had to leave with his eleven sons and their families to live in Egypt as foreigners and aliens. It took them four hundred years before they were able to leave their refugee camps and become immigrants again in another land that God had prepared for them.

- Joseph was the original "dreamer" with his own dream coat to boot.

- After Assyria's destruction and dispersion of the ten northern tribes of Israel, only the two southern tribes of Judah remained. And then the Babylonians took Judah a few years later. It was seventy-five years before the Jews were allowed to return to Jerusalem.

God understands displaced people. Aliens, immigrants, and dreamers are part of the grander biblical narrative. The notion of displacement is more the standard throughout history, not the norm. So what lessons, if any, can we learn from these stories and apply to today's situations?

In the Old Testament, Leviticus 19:34

instructs Israel on the treatment of aliens. This passage admonished Jews to treat foreigners fairly and not to forget that they, too, had been aliens while in Egypt. The first thing that strikes me is that living as an alien helps someone to appreciate what aliens go through in a strange land. And how to treat them.

Let's pick this up in the New Testament, which refers to Christ's followers as aliens and strangers whose true and ultimate place of inhabitance is heaven (1 Peter 2:11–12). The more I read about what *alien* and *immigrant* mean in Scripture, I find that it's more of a mentality than a geographically displaced individual. I think that's why Scripture has so much to say about the disenfranchised and uses the metaphor of Christ's followers as foreigners in a strange land.

I really believe that our nation is having so much trouble with these issues today because the further we move away from Scripture and its tenets and principles, the less likely we will embody the ethos contained in its pages. American society may have been *more* welcoming of its strangers when it was *more* welcoming of Scripture.

The more we remove the Bible from the marketplace of ideas, the less we will exemplify what it teaches. Safety and security are some of the key reasons many people want to return to an isolationist policy. I certainly understand the issues surrounding terrorism today. Sound policy must accompany the political will to fulfill one of the prime roles of government, which is to assure the safety of its people. But can sound policy and humanitarian need come together in wise decision-making? I believe it can, but it will take those not driven by agendas to make it happen. It will happen only when decision makers also see themselves as aliens and immigrants and act from that baseline of thinking.

The bigger the political debate on this issue, the more we need to focus on what I call the "transcendence of immigration." And I find no greater illustration of the transcendence of immigration than in the person of Jesus. Talk about a "dreamer." A child born in a manger in a foreign land that his parents traveled to. Sounds much like the dreamers of today. The very notion of God stepping out of eternity into time to live among us is the ultimate immigration story, and Jesus was the ultimate immigrant.

Jesus was the ultimate immigrant.

Scripture says that Jesus came so all of us could experience the wonder of God's love, which created a new community of people who understood and accepted their roles as aliens in this world. They looked to their God as the One who calmed their fears amid turbulence, political unrest, and dislike of their people group.

Jesus constantly was changing the ground rules about who our neighbor is, how we treat others, how we envision our security, and how to be a good citizen. His entire Sermon on the Mount was a counterintuitive manifesto for this new community of displaced people. Jesus came to define this new community as one comprised of immigrants and aliens living in their *own* land. Their displacement was of the spirit and not one of geography. To best understand the immigrant mentality, we must identify first as an immigrant. It's a spiritual exercise to transcend the physical world's perspective and grasp a new identity as an alien.

This new community was radical to the core. Jesus empowered women, healed the sick, and welcomed children—giving hope to the weak, the poor, and the enslaved. He focused on the outcasts and the disenfranchised, like lepers—the unclean citizenry of his day, relegated to their own refugee camps. A leper running among the clean was the terrorist of his day.

The world had never seen or heard of the things he embodied. He taught us a new definition of community—simply that others would know everyone who believed in him by one thing: their love for one another. He invited everyone to be a part of this community; there were no distinctions. He helped everyone understand that, to a degree, we are all refugees, aliens, or immigrants. When we understand that, our neighbor begins to look less like the bad guy and more like a brother.

That's what the gospel *looks* like when its adherents act it out in the name of Jesus, which leads me to this point: *the inclusiveness of the gospel best illustrates the exclusiveness of its design.* Everyone is welcome. Because everyone is a refugee. We are all in the same boat on the way to the heavenly shore. That's the inclusiveness of the message. And yet it's exclusive to the people who embrace it.

America will become good again when we unfriend all the rhetoric of fear, scapegoating, and political wrangling over who our neighbors are. Look into the eyes and heart of Jesus and find your peace there. When you do, you will find your neighbor as well.

Chapter 6

Poverty

In recent memory, one of the editorial hallmarks of the Gulf War was the embedded journalist. We heard and saw war firsthand as it happened. Nothing like being involved and on-site to best understand what people experience. It's the same thing in life. Being embedded allows us to be more accurate than speaking from a distance or from the sideline. Intersection helps us in our dissection of experiences.

I learned that lesson very well after my graduation from Boston University, when I returned home to North Jersey to begin my career in journalism. As part of a desire to further my education, I enrolled in a rather unique program offered through New York Seminary called the Urban Theological Year, taught by noted urban church planter Dr. Bill Iverson. The emphasis of the course was to prepare people for understanding urban street mentality in order to better interpret it. Coming from my rather comfortable middle-class Italian family model, this was certainly something outside my life experience. As a journalist and as a Christian, I felt it would offer me a perspective on life that would serve me well as an interpreter of the social sphere—something I knew very little about.

That year, we explored many topics totally foreign to my worldview, like black liberation theology and the politics of poverty, among others. Really interesting discussions transpired among our ethnically and racially diverse group of recent college grads whom Dr. Iverson had assembled from around the country to meet in his home in Orange, New Jersey. We were a ragtag bunch. White. Black. Asian. Chicano. Southern rednecks. Ex-hippies. It took almost six months for us just to break down the walls between us! But it was worth it. In the end, it was one of the greatest learning experiences of my life.

The first lesson I learned was that getting outside yourself is the foundation of true learning. I often like to say that we cannot look inward to find what can only be found outside us. One particular assignment was quite outside the box for me, as well as for the rest of the team. Dr. Iverson assigned each of us to live in a rescue mission in Manhattan for one weekend. We would experience what others who entered a mission on a Friday night experienced, and we would not tell anyone who we were, not even the director or staff at the mission. Our objective was simply to observe, interact with the fellow indigents with whom we lived, and then report our observations to the group.

Okay. I could do that. In order to look somewhat indigent myself, I didn't shave for a week, found the oldest clothes I had to wear, and went into Manhattan early that Friday to walk around in the rain to smell somewhat musty before heading to the mission. When I got to the mission, I stood in line with all the others waiting for a hot meal and a roof over their heads for the weekend. And that's when the lesson of becoming embedded began.

As I stood there, I got into a conversation with an out-of-town man who decided to engage a prostitute in his car overnight in a no-parking zone. The police discovered them and impounded his car, and it would cost him $300 to retrieve it from the pound. Well, he had no money left after paying a fine for his indiscretion, so he could not get the car and return home. So there he was at the mission. It became obvious that he didn't know how he was going to come up with $300, which was a lot of money in 1973.

This conversation was quite foreign to me. I asked him why he didn't just call someone in his family to help him out. Or, if that was too embarrassing, go find a temporary job doing anything to make the money. And then I learned an important truth about the mindset of poverty. It's one thing to be poor; it's another thing to be poor *and* hopeless. People who have lost hope have lost way more than the ability to look for a job. They have lost the ability to believe that anyone would hire them. Worse yet, the accompanying feeling is that no one cares anyway. The real issue is not finding a job; it's recovering the meaning to life that enables someone to believe that work is valuable to one's identity and self-esteem. The two ideas go hand in hand to forge character. As I stood there talking to that man, I began to realize that poverty of spirit had assigned him to a caste system, and he believed he was unable to break out of the system.

We see the politics of poverty all around us. Politicians all say they want to create jobs without knowing or caring to know that providing a job is only good if you provide hope as well. Poverty of the pocket is one side of the coin. Poverty of the spirit is the other. When both needs are met, a person has a much better chance of breaking cycles and strongholds.

My next lesson came a few hours later after the evening meal. My mother was a great Italian cook. On her very worst day, I never in my life tasted anything like I had that night. I still don't know what it was. Then after the meal, everyone had to take a shower. They took our clothes and hung them in a room to fumigate them to kill the lice because they never knew where any of these people might have been while living on the streets. Everyone received what seemed like a hospital gown to wear for the rest of the evening and to bed.

But the most important lesson was soon to come. There was a man playing chess by himself, and I enjoyed the game, so I asked him if I could play. There was nothing else to do. It was not like there were flat-screen TVs with unlimited channels of entertainment. He nodded, and I joined him. And for two hours we played chess. We did not exchange a word between us. Usually I can strike up a conversation with anyone. Not this time. I learned the sense of anonymity that poverty of the spirit breeds. And anonymity leads to invisibility. That man felt invisible. With no identity and no hope, he was a ghost to everyone around him.

That weekend in the mission did more to help me understand the politics of poverty than anything I have ever done, read, or heard since. Walking a mile in those shoes opened my eyes to how people should treat one another (and why there are no easy answers to anyone's problems without involvement). It also revealed to me that until I intersect with people in *that* situation, my understanding is inadequate. The same is true for anyone who likes to say what people need without experiencing how they feel. All that does is spread misinformation and fuel our hubris, tricking us into thinking that we've contributed something positive to the national narrative on this topic.

Social media is notorious for this kind of grandstanding. Trying to understand the world through social media without intersection is nothing but misinformed opinion. It allows us to speak from a vacuum of thought and to say whatever we choose without any repercussion. And boy, so many have so much to say about things they know nothing about. As I often say, people like to speak with authority out of ignorance.

> Jesus restores hope to those who feel unloved and uncared for.

That's why we must look to Jesus as our model for intersection, which gives an expression to the face of humanity. When he walked the earth, he allowed people to touch the hem of his garment, he went to the home of someone whose daughter just died, and he went to a tomb to cry over a friend's death. Still today, Jesus restores hope to those who feel unloved and uncared for. And above all else, Jesus leads everyone to the cross, which is the greatest level playing field of all time. And he died for us. It's hard to feel unloved and uncared for when someone goes to that length to show his love. Now that is the ultimate form of intersection that we cannot achieve through a Facebook post or a tweet or anything written in a blog. Your intersection in the lives of those around you can be the encouragement they need to break free from their poverty of the spirit and their culture of anonymity. Consider embedding yourself in an environment totally foreign to your worldview. God refuels us not to stay in the garage but to become his vehicles of change.

America will become good again when we unfriend the tendency to misinform because of our lack of involvement.

Chapter 7

GREEN THINKING

All of us are in search of happiness and the peace that comes with it. We all know clichés like "money can't buy you happiness." And we know that an attitude of thankfulness fosters contentment.

Happiness does not necessarily occur by chance, as we can take specific actions in our lives to create it. I read something about happiness by author, TV show host, *Psychology Today* blogger, and corporate trainer Robert Puff, PhD, who's been studying and writing about human achievement for decades. I think he hits the nail on the head about one of the key ways to attain happiness.

When people call him for advice, he suggests that they "go for a walk for thirty minutes to an hour and focus on being present with the outdoors. If after their walk, they still feel just as despondent, then they should give me another call. The result? In nearly twenty-five years, I've rarely received the second call."[2]

He continues, "When we identify with the present moment and focus on the beauty that surrounds us, we increase happiness. When our minds are still, fully present with the here-and-now, and without the mental commentary, then we experience a peace that surpasses understanding. Go outside and find a place where you're not

2   Robert Puff, "Two Key Steps to Finding Happiness," *Psychology Today*, May 9, 2012, https://www.psychologytoday.com/us/blog/meditation-modern-life/201205/two-key-steps-finding-happiness.

surrounded by many people. This may be a park, meadow, lake, or beach. Find an object to focus on, such as a flower, tree, bird, or water. For one to ten minutes, draw all of your attention onto what you've chosen to focus on. Listen to it, watch it, just be with it. Resist the urge to analyze it or create a story about it."

Kudos to you, Dr. Puff, for your insight into one of the great mysteries of life! You've identified the right environment where one can begin to understand how the universe works and how God created us to fit into that model.

I'm going to ask this question to illustrate what the Bible and Dr. Puff tell us: Did you ever wonder why God called it the garden of Eden and not the city of Eden? Why did God choose to place Adam and Eve in a garden and not in a city? Answer: Because being around God's creation points to God and peace more than being in an environment stripped of God. God creates nature, and man creates anti-nature.

To me, the issue of climate change is so fraught with political dialogue that it's hard to see behind it to a larger issue—that we must be the stewards of our earth that God demanded of us. When I want to find out nature's best plan for humans to experience peace and fulfillment, I usually go to Scripture. There are many life principles that we can mine from the riches in that book.

So what principles do I find built around the perfect environment of Eden that enable me to find happiness? Let me illustrate my answer by telling you a story about my childhood.

I love spring—the time of year when we come out of winter hibernation and colors once again come alive all around us. What a reminder that life has beauty if we only take the time to see it. Smell it. Walk in it.

This came home to me once during a conversation with friends. As we talked about health, nutrition, and overall spiritual health, somehow the topic turned to how much I have always enjoyed working in a garden. This part of my built-in DNA, I believe, stems from my Italian heritage but also from the many hours I spent working in the rather large garden we had at home. My grandfather, uncle, father, brother, and I would tend it.

When my grandfather was alive, he would prepare the entire garden—almost ten thousand square feet—by hand with a pitchfork. Of course, he was used to hard work because that's all he ever knew. It seemed that extreme perspiration was part of being Italian, which may explain why I became a journalist. (After my grandfather passed away, my father and uncle decided to move closer to the twentieth century and get a rototiller to do all that work.)

I never feel more content and at peace than when I'm sitting in the dirt on a sunny summer day, planting tomatoes, cucumbers, and squash, among others. Like I said, I think Dr. Puff hit the nail on the head with his comments about spending time outdoors. Being one with nature is very much a biblical principle for several reasons.

The psalmist declares that the heavens reveal the glory of the Lord (Psalm 19:1). In Romans, Paul reminds us that God reveals his handiwork in nature and in the heavens (1:20). Jesus alludes to God's care and presence in his creation when he asks us to trust and not worry about today, for he clothes the flowers of the field and provides food for the birds (Matthew 6:25–34).

Yes, there is an undeniable link between the God of the universe and the universe itself, just as artists have a spiritual connection with their art and often create art that reflects what's deep in their souls. Nature is God's silent language to us that reveals much about his character. We see order, beauty, purpose, and breathtaking majesty, as well as force and power and even destruction. To me, it's evident that nature reveals much about the existence of God. So to remove elements of the creation (clean air, trees, grass, lakes and rivers, and creatures) is to remove those very things that God created to bear witness to himself. When we surround ourselves with less of God's creation, we remove an aspect of God's presence from our lives. As such, the Christ-follower should be the most ardent of all conservationists.

But if we strip away the things of nature that by design communicate a sense of order, tranquility, and transcendence, then society will gravitate toward the antithesis of those things—disorder, stress, and focus on self, which breeds selfishness. Without a God to embrace, we feel hardwired to create our own gods to fill the vacuum in our souls.

I believe the trend toward urban gardening and the increase in millennials leaving the corporate world in favor of organic farming careers (according to recent stats by the U.S. Department of Agriculture) is fueled by an innate drive in people to experience the peace of God in the midst of the urban culture that sucks life from us and from our spirits.

The movement in the eighteenth and nineteenth centuries to build parks in the middle of urban environments—Central Park in New York being the most notable—came about precisely to provide people with a glimpse of God and an opportunity for citizens to retreat, refuel, and relax. And the great architects of these parks and gardens, for the most part, were biblicists.

> Be still and focus on God's creation.

So if you're feeling far from God, step away from the emptiness of the online creation and take a trip to the country. Be still and focus on God's creation, as Dr. Puff suggests. Better yet, put on some old clothes and go sit in the dirt and plant some tomatoes. Listen to the voice of God in the wind as it whips through the trees. Feel his presence in the warmth of the sun. Pray. Sing a worship song. I'll bet you will feel a lot better at the end of the day.

America will become good again when we choose not to lose ourselves in the debate of climate change to the detriment of a larger issue, which is the human role in fostering an attitude of stewardship and appreciation for all created life. When we embrace that perspective, our desire to protect the planet will change as well.

Chapter 8

Gun Control

Scripture claims that there's a moral fabric to the universe, sort of a universal moral compass that God has built into the DNA of each person (Romans chapters 1 and 2). And with that moral compass comes a common-sense approach to and interaction with our world. If I understand what Jesus is saying, it's that we lose our common sense when we lose our God-given moral compass.

The further individuals and societies stray from a biblical morality, the more their common-sense approach to life declines. That's why there are so many examples of people exhibiting a lack of common sense in our culture. We have replaced common sense with nonsense.

> We lose our common sense when we lose our God-given moral compass.

To offset this growing lack of common sense, Jesus calls us to be counter-culturalists in our response to society, much like he was during his time on earth. As society moves farther away from God's laws, Jesus asks us to remain centered by following that moral compass residing deeply within us. Not only does this keep us from becoming lost, but it also allows people who are desperate to find their true north.

Jesus also asks his followers to focus on how to relate to each other and to society in general, both of which are often counterintuitive. Jesus' examples of counterintuitive thinking are every-where in the Bible. Take, for instance, "Whoever finds his life will lose it, and whoever loses his life for my sake will find it" (Matthew 10:39 ESV). Or "The last will be first, and the first will be last" (Matthew 20:16 NIV). These statements are coun-terintuitive because they defy the current moral direction of self-aggrandizement.

But Jesus also said that one could discern counterintuitive spiritual principles by having wis-dom. They do not simply come with knowledge or through human understanding. Psalm 111:10 says, "The fear of the Lord is the beginning of wis-dom" (NIV). That's where it starts. As our soci-ety becomes more secular, it would have us look to ourselves to establish truth, but Jesus says the opposite: he is the truth. Truth and the wisdom of God do not exist within us until we invite him into our hearts. We must look outside of ourselves and to the person of Christ. Only then can we live in the power of the Holy Spirit.

Common sense is only common when our moral compasses are working. Strip away the moral compass, and you lose access to common sense. They work hand in hand. Because we've looked inwardly at our human understanding to determine our own moral compass, our society has paid a high price. How? The more we look inwardly, the more fear we sense. Stop there and ponder that statement for a minute. Yes, I said the more we try to define our own truth, the more evident fear will become in our lives and in our corporate culture. Why? Because we cannot answer the great questions of life by looking inside ourselves. We cannot find within us that which only exists when we accept God's truth. Our society is now experiencing the results of this exaggerated inward perspective—a generation of confused individuals who are looking for truth inside themselves.

One blatantly obvious result of this phenomenon is our violent society. Without a moral compass, we are adrift on the way to nowhere. That lack of true north breeds fear. Fear breeds anger and isolation. Did you ever stop to think why there is such an increase in violence in our public spaces? The answer might simply be that we are afraid and hopeless. Fear breeds anger, and anger is what we see play out every day in our news.

This brings us to where we are today on the issue of gun control in America. As a society, we need to examine the terrible increase in violent crimes in our schools against innocent children of all ages more closely and honestly. We try to understand the sheer insanity of someone coming into a school, a theater, or an open-air concert venue with weapons to summarily kill innocent individuals. Of course, we can't, because acts like these are outside the realm of anything sensible. We are searching for reason in acts that are utterly unreasonable.

Let me suggest that the issue is not simply a

matter of people owning guns. I do not own a gun. I never have, but I have no problem with those who do. But for the life of me, I cannot understand the almost pathological irrationality of gun advocates who cannot agree to wait a few days for thorough background checks on individuals who purchase a gun. I mean, it took me three days to get my new refrigerator recently. And a week to get my new car. I can't wait a day to get my gun? I'm sorry, but that thinking eludes me.

It's also irrational and not very scientific to blame violence on people having guns. People have always had guns, and they did not act like they do today. What's changed in the equation of society's makeup that now causes people to use those weapons like never before on the most innocent and vulnerable among us?

When you conduct an experiment in an effort to understand why something occurs in nature, you add variables into those environments until you find a probable cause. The question we should be asking is, "What's new to our culture that may be the cause of our corporate angst, which has turned people into mass murderers at an alarming rate?" Certainly, it's not merely having a gun. Or mental illnesses. Both have been in our environment for some time. So, what then is the probable cause?

To ask that question and seek an honest answer, we'd have to have an intellectually honest discourse. A discourse that political correctness does not allow because we would have to introduce the notion of a moral law beyond the laws we make ourselves. And to agree to a moral law beyond us, we'd have to agree that there is a God. Therein lies the problem. We can't do that because we'd offend all the atheists. And truthfully, many of us like being our own gods.

The answer may be that when we stripped away the moral compass and lost our common sense, we became morally blind. You can see the effect of this moral blindness everywhere. The blindness is pandemic. Reality shows (or "surreality," as I've called them) are rampant with people acting in ways that reflect no shame, no responsibility, and no character. Maybe the first step to gun control is control of ourselves.

The good news is that Jesus healed the blind two thousand years ago, and he can do so again today. He asks us to receive our sight from him and become the countercultural and counterintuitive agents to this world who will bring light and healing to those headed in the wrong direction without their true north. When we do this and ask people to look outside of themselves to find their way (Jesus said he was *the* way in John 14:6), their fear will subside as well. And anger will turn to calm. Then we can hear Jesus' voice above the nonsense saying, "Come to me, all you who are weary and burdened, and I will give you rest" (Matthew 11:28 NIV).

Jesus promises us a light yoke when we harness ourselves to him and he is in control of our lives. The world promises us no yoke or harness and calls that *freedom*. Really? Freedom to be adrift on the way to nowhere? To be fearful? To constantly be searching for the more and more we hear will satisfy us? But it never does. Is that really the freedom we long for? We've seen how this freedom has impacted our culture negatively, with violence rather than love.

America will become good again when we embrace fullness of life without being full of ourselves. Talk about an easier way to live.

Chapter 9

FAKE NEWS

I'm a card-carrying member of the media. I've spent my life and career in New York and worked with some very talented broadcasters, writers, producers, and journalists.

I happen to believe that one of the greatest careers one can choose is journalism. This comment may be a bit self-serving, as my training happens to be in journalism, which I pursued immediately after graduating from Boston University. Due to certain providential circumstances in my life, I soon found myself as a broadcaster, and that's where my career took me. But I have always felt I had the heart of a journalist and still enjoy writing as an avocation. I have taught journalism and have a deep respect for the classic role of the journalist, which is to interpret the social sphere and, as I define it, "illumine what others cannot see."

Fast-forward to our current cultural fixation on the new term that defines the illegitimate child of classic journalism: "fake news." Popularized to the point of absurdity in the last election, the very idea of fake news has played a key role in the alarmingly growing percentage of Americans who distrust the media to present researched and factual observations and interpretations of the news.

Journalism used to be all about observation and interpretation. Today, it seems to be fraught with titillation and misinformation, playing to a growing addiction to voyeurism, for which the internet has been quite responsible in this unseemly metamorphosis. The internet has become the preferred sandbox and playground for anyone who chooses to question everything and make statements about anything or anyone without any shred of evidence or corroborating testimony of first-person accounts.

Nowadays, many people consider themselves journalists by virtue of their attempts to interpret their social sphere via their preferred choice of social media, in whatever uncivil language they choose to use. You can say anything you want, as facts seem to be afterthoughts rather than central to the process. It's real-time observation with no context, no accountability for what one does, and no desire to be accurate in the presentation.

The journalist's responsibility has always been to state nothing more than the truth and nothing less than the truth. Anything other than that is not the truth. It's an agenda—a mentality that spawned the fake-news syndrome. And it seems as if everyone has an agenda today. This trend toward unrestricted inhibition has allowed people to assume the role of self-appointed online spokespeople for whatever agenda they want to propose. No one needs to be right; they just need a platform.

To begin with, fake news cannot exist in an environment that believes in the search for truth. One of the greatest examples of fake news in history occurred when religious leaders brought Jesus to Pilate with less-than-accurate accusations and trumped-up charges. Pilate confronted Jesus, the person who claimed to be "the truth" (John 14:6), asking, "What is truth?" (18:38)—the same question we ask today.

You see, fake news is not new. It's always been around and will always be around as long as people do not want to face that which is true, obvious, and uncomfortable. It's always more expedient to give life to a lie than to put your ego to death.

Jesus came to enable us to face our own death to self. Ironically, he called that freedom.

If we are to find freedom today in the midst of fake news, we cannot hide behind the firewall of impersonality found on the internet. Fake environments must come up with fake news to legitimize their fake community. When we put our faith in that which is not real, the result is usually not very real either. There is so much fake news online that it's hard to tell the difference between the real and surreal, deception and misconception, delusion and illusion. Truth is disappearing quicker than the magician's sleight of hand. I firmly believe that the antidote to all this is to restore each of us to true community—to relationships that will demand integrity, walk in truthfulness, and challenge inauthenticity. The fake communities, whether online or anywhere, will never accomplish that with people who demand nothing from each other but fodder for more controversy and confusion.

The challenge for each of us is to loosen the

grip these communities have on us for more con-sumption of that which is not real. Jesus came to give us the good news all the time. He promises us a community of people who will demand more of themselves than others demand of them and strive for that which is true because he is the truth. And "the truth will set you free" (John 8:32 ESV).

There's a measure of intellectual honesty when you state what is obvious . . . because it's obvious. And if it's not so obvious, you do your best to describe what you're seeing, not what you want to see. Which led me to my definition of jour-nalism: "To illumine what others cannot see." Now, let's turn the page to where we find ourselves in our current politically correct world that asks us to not state the obvious because it might offend someone or rub a certain group of people the wrong way.

Media personalities have now become seeth-ing advocates of ideology, not truth. Their mantra seems to be: "State your position. Defend it even if it's not true or applicable to the situation. Argue to make yourself heard. Not because you have something to say but because you have nothing to say." Whether liberal or conservative, it's equally distasteful. This is beyond partisan anything. Our media is in danger of embracing the same *noblesse oblige* attitude toward the masses as the leadership in Washington. This attitude is insulting. The hoi polloi can no longer figure out anything for themselves. We now must put up with the self-appointed interpreters of what is apparent. We now treat each other as if we are fragile, all ideas are equal, and some contemporary thought is only as chic as those who promulgate it. It's the PC thinking *de jour*: it need not be accurate nor exhibit common sense as long as it is popular.

Tragically, we now look for truth in dung heaps. We stick our hand in the muck, pull it out, and hold up what we've grabbed. Then we admire it and declare it relevant and believable. And woe to those who have not drunk the Kool-Aid and still have a modicum of common sense to look at it in disbelief and say openly, "It's just a pile of dung." It's hard to refrain from using the more expletive synonym here. Those who disagree with the PC nonsense are excoriated because they are not in lockstep with the thought of the day that truth no longer matters. Or even exists. The obvious is no longer obvious, and to state the obvious would fly in the face of the approved political-speak of the day advocated by the self-appointed gatekeepers of the American lexicon.

But that's not new. Jesus had to confront his version of the media elite of his day, those who were the communicators of all that was supposed to be evident and true to the masses in need of explanations. These were the self-proclaimed righteous religious rulers who acted as the journalists and who were more interested in sustaining their versions of reality than in telling people the truth.

Jesus steps into this arena and begins to help people see beyond the political-speak to what is real in the kingdom of God. In the Sermon on the

Mount, Jesus used that platform to interpret life and truth in a language different from what everyone traditionally heard from the communicators of the day. He certainly fit my definition of the journalist—the One who can illumine what others cannot see. He interpreted how to live life in the "blessed are you" comments about the meek, the poor in spirit, the hungry, etc.

This was a new kind of truth, stripped of the politically correct speak of his day because it went beyond all that rhetoric. It stated things that neither Caesar nor the ruling Jewish elite could grasp. Jesus redefined the ground rules and brought new definition to life's experiences. He is still doing that today. He wants to redefine the PC speak of our day, so we no longer have to scrounge in dung heaps to find truth like much of our media asks us to do. Jesus said he was the truth and went on to say that the truth would set you free (John 8:32).

He also asks us to be perfect, as our heavenly Father is perfect (Matthew 5:48). Interestingly, he states this at the end of the section about loving our enemies because there's nothing harder than forgiving the people who want to harm you. So he picks the hardest thing for us to humanly do in order to be perfect. Why do you think he did that? He did it to show us that we simply cannot be perfect. He points us to the need and then says he will be the One to help us meet that need.

> We can find freedom when we find Jesus.

The good news is that we can find freedom when we find Jesus. All the politically correct speak of the day that asks us to accept absurdity as reality flies in the face of the words of Jesus. He is our logos, the highest form of truth and logic, and he asks each of us to simply look at life through the grid he provided. When we do, we find freedom, rest, love, forgiveness, and charity. These are the fruits of a life hidden in his truth. The aroma that

Jesus leaves us with when he presents his truth is sweet. It's filled with peace and grace. The world offers us dung. Jesus offers us the aroma of life. Choose wisely.

America will become good again when we reject the PC speak of the day that asks us to accept whatever it pulls from the dung heap. Let's just say what it is and that it smells!

Chapter 10

THE CULTURE WAR

When I was a kid, the Cold War was at its height. It was the United States against the Soviet Union. We exported democracy, and the USSR exported communism. East against West. They wore the black hats. We wore the white ones. It was easy to tell who the enemy was. Our cartoons even exploited it. Boris and Natasha against Rocky and Bullwinkle. They called it "the Cold War" because of the frozen stalemate between the two superpowers. No one was really fighting each other. It was one big standoff, fraught with innuendo, threats of nuclear war, bluster, and bluffing. Americans united against this common threat.

Fast forward a generation. After the fall of the Berlin Wall and the seeming defeat of communism, we thought the war was over. Then a new war arose—only this time it pitted Americans against each other. In this new war, the enemy did not have a face. Instead, it was an ideology filled with the same godlessness as the Communists and deemed so terrible that leaders of some evangelical camps assembled a coalition to fight it. Mailing lists were compiled, people recruited, rhetoric established, and sides chosen. Called "the Culture War," it's been going on for a while without signs of it coming to an end.

But if you have a war, you must also have an enemy. The two go together like fire and heat. You can't have one without the other. But Jesus was very clear that his followers only have one real enemy, and they were not the Roman rulers of the day, unfair legislation, religious hypocrisy, or lack of social justice.

Simply put, culture wars are not new. Jesus faced one when he was alive, and we face ours today. He wanted his disciples then and now to understand that pitting people against each other is inherently not his style. He still calls on his people to see beyond this world and to fight neither Caesar nor the Jewish leaders. The liberals nor the conservatives. The Republicans nor the Democrats. He has no affiliation.

In the political arena, we can celebrate those who affirm biblical principles and work to implement laws that reflect those principles. We can also call them out when their actions and speech do not model Christ's behavior. Sadly, our current president in 2020 is often worthy of both. In a political sense, there is a very real need to challenge actions and ideas that are absent of biblical truth and morality. To turn a blind eye would be a disservice to the country, the Constitution which protects its citizenry with irrefutable biblical nobility, and the calling many hear from Christ to serve him in that arena.

> As Christians, our objective is to help each other become better humans, not better political allies.

Similarly, a spiritual obligation exists for believers. To overlook anyone whose actions and language are noticeably absent of Christ-like behavior is a disservice to the cause of Christ. He calls us to a higher standard, and we must be as honest and diligent to call each other out in the spirit of accountability as we would anyone else, especially those who dare to bear the name of Christ-follower. Ends never justify the means in the economy of the kingdom of God. When our heads tell us one thing, our hearts must remember that we no longer live, but Christ lives in us. Iron can only sharpen iron when they are rubbed together. As Christians, our objective is to help each other become better humans, not better political allies.

Ultimately, the government is not the savior of the American society. If we believe so, it's all too easy to lose sight of what and whom we uplift to respect and follow. It's easy to replace one savior with another one. Jesus said in the book of John, "I, when I am lifted up from the earth, will draw all people to myself" (12:32 NIV). Not through the uplifting of his words nor the uplifting of his choice for a political party. And not even the uplifting of one of his disciples and best representatives. Jesus is our north star, not a political party or platform favorable to the politically correct Christian agenda.

No, he pointed to *himself* to be lifted up. There is one very important lesson to learn from Scripture and history: when we raise the flag higher than the cross, we have a problem. When that happens, people get confused as to which Jesus we're talking about. Jesus divorced himself from taking sides because he knew that taking sides only leads to an *us-versus-them* mentality. It creates trench warfare where we simply remain holed up in our foxholes of belief, preferring to lob verbal grenades and mortars into each other's camps and take on casualties.

As evangelicals, we often use our faith as our excuse to quickly denounce those who would stand against our biblical worldview. It's one thing to disagree and another to angrily contend in the marketplace with mean spirits toward those with whom we disagree. As best I can determine, Jesus wants his followers not only to lift him up in all that we say and do but also in the *way* we say it and do it. He points to himself as the Savior with all humility and exhibits true power by going to the cross. Jesus wants us to understand that the only hill worth dying on is Calvary. When we set up other hills to die for, we miss the mindset of Jesus.

America will become good again when we refuse to fight the "Culture War" and remember who the real enemy is. Otherwise, those who might really see Jesus in you will get confused about the gospel when you raise the flag higher than the cross.

Section 3

RISING ABOVE

Chapter 11

Forgiveness: An Answer to the Culture War

Our diet of news consumption tells us there's an awful lot of bad going on out there. It's hard to tell the difference between the good guys and the bad guys. The lines are so blurry that what society once considered bad is now good. And vice versa. The template for determining either is now up to you, as standards of absolute truth are no longer simply blurry; they have vanished from the minds of many. You can find examples of that everywhere online. One of the most glaring examples of blurred vision has to do with finding fault with everything and everyone based only on the standard you hold up as being the benchmark for right and wrong. One thing is for certain: when you read what's on the web, you won't see a whole lot of forgiveness.

True community, however, will exemplify forgiveness as one of the resounding traits of its existence, as well as the ability to unify people rather than divide them, which is more of what the internet feeds us. The web acts as a form of modern-day trench warfare, as we lob verbal and printed grenades on each page we surf. We have become adept at division, and I'm not talking about math.

Everyone is upset about something. A spirit of unforgiveness is running rampant in our land, and it's consuming us. The internet fosters this spirit, and we must consider the alternative to extinguish this wildfire of the tongue before it burns our entire land with bitterness. That alternative is true community, where we can extinguish unforgiveness and the power it has over us for good.

> Love may question and forgive,
> but it does not judge.

Starting in John 8:15, Jesus gives us a good picture of why forgiveness is important. And why judgment is not ours to take. Apparently, judgment is so weighty that both the Father and Son must agree. So when you and I judge, we usurp the role relegated solely to the prerogative of God. Which is why our judgment is void of love, as it has nothing of the Spirit of God invested in the pronouncement. Love may question and forgive, but it does not judge. Our social media landscape, on the other hand, is littered with unforgiveness, judgment, and condemnation.

In Matthew 6, Jesus teaches his disciples a little prayer that may be the most well-known prayer in Western civilization. We all know it as the "Our Father." It starts off simply enough, "Our Father, which art in heaven." Then it takes off from there to reveal something deeply profound.

If you carefully look at what Jesus asked us to pray, this simple prayer was giving us a glimpse of the heavenly *modus operandi* for enjoying a quality of life here on earth. He meant to have us look outside ourselves and beyond our circumstances to God's heavenly kingdom as the focal point for understanding our earthly existence. The mystery and the opportunity are that we can experience now on earth the same kind of relationship that is experienced in heaven. They are one and the same. Stop and think about that for a minute.

Forgiveness reflects the heavenly visage. Forgiveness works because it reflects the heart of God. Jesus came to forgive, not to condemn. The more our society blurs who God is, the more we blur our understanding of who our brother is. Jesus says that heaven is the frame of reference for earthly living. He then adds several more similarities between the two kingdoms. And here's where it really gets interesting. One is forgiveness. The other is to eschew temptations that emanate from the evil one.

Forgiveness is a central theme because it's integral for entering and enjoying God's kingdom, so it's important to begin that lesson on earth. We practice here and now for the real thing later on. We get a glimpse of it on earth and see it fully in action in heaven because only the forgiven and those who forgave will be there (Matthew 6:14–15). When put into practice, it has power to transform.

The most highly publicized example of that in our modern time is how Nelson Mandela exemplified the power of forgiveness to unite South Africa after his release from prison and ascension to the highest political platform in the land. For many years, he languished in a South African prison, a victim of that nation's apartheid policy. He was a political prisoner in the truest sense of the word. That experience usually embitters a man to the point of no return. Instead, that prison became the crucible for refining his character to embody the one trait that would define him to the world and change his country. That one thing was forgiveness.

Few people have embodied the power of that concept in our time as Mandela. Which is why he was such a powerful force for change. He modeled what Jesus taught, especially his little prayer in which heaven is the frame of reference for earthly living (Matthew 6:9–13). Mandela caught a glimpse of that heavenly frame of reference while in prison, which forged his view of the eternal. He came to understand the power of forgiveness to release us from ourselves, as well as from a jail cell, and to help us resist the temptation to exact revenge. Lack of forgiveness only leads one back to self-interest. And self-interest closes the gates to real freedom. Mandela learned that true forgiveness has the power to transform one person—or an entire society.

Mandela's imprisonment refined his focus so that he learned to see more clearly. He would not let the temptations of revenge or bitterness cloud his vision for uniting his nation. He knew forgiveness was the one tool that would best forge this new nation. He wanted to see the kingdom of heaven exemplified in his beloved South Africa. In doing so, Mandela became a microcosm of life in heaven right here on earth when he chose forgiveness over hate and vengeance.

We, too, can choose the same path as Mandela. Our world desperately needs to see forgiveness instead of retribution. For a moment, the world saw it in Charleston after the shooting that claimed nine lives at the Emmanuel AME Church in June 2015. Several days after the shooting, with the assailant apprehended, family members and friends lined up to say they forgave the shooter. What? Forgive the shooter? The executioner of innocent people? Their testimony stopped us in our tracks. It seemed . . . unnatural. Yet somehow, in our hearts, it also seemed like the right thing to do.

On the other hand, if we continue to assign blame to all the wrongs of the world—whether to rogue cops, terrorist groups, corrupt politicians—we will never experience peace in our society. Or even peace in ourselves. We can reflect on Mandela's life and find the power of interpreting the heavenly kingdom on earth. If so, then forgiveness will be the hallmark of our lives "on earth as it is in heaven" (v. 10). That's something that we can only achieve by personal sacrifice, as we live out lives in community to exhibit that type of power.

Another thing about withholding forgiveness: it keeps us imprisoned and outside the kingdom and the joys that we can experience on earth. Self-aggrandizement follows this kind of lifestyle. The more we focus on ourselves, the less we can focus on forgiveness. These two tie together in some mystical way and reinforce the other. That's why Jesus focuses so strongly on these two elements of how to achieve kingdom living. There is no resisting of temptation without forgiveness and no forgiveness without resisting the efforts of the evil one, who uses temptations as cataracts over the heavenly vision.

America will become good again when we reject a spirit of unforgiveness and embrace an attitude of forgiveness as the hallmark of our life here on earth . . . as it is in heaven. Amen.

Chapter 12

Reaffirming Our Roots

If you happen to take a short drive north of San Francisco, you'll run into one of the great natural treasures of our country: the California redwood forest. The sizes of those coniferous trees are legendary and stunning. It's hard to imagine that one of those trees grew from some little seed.

You would think that the very size of those redwoods would dictate that each one must have a huge underground root system to keep it from top-pling over during a major storm. To the contrary, they have a very shallow root system. The one thing that saves the trees from falling is that the root systems become so intertwined that all the trees connect as a group to support each individual one.

Now that sounds like a real community. It's all about the roots. A strong foundation with connections to others enhances the overall strength of a community to help everyone withstand whatever forces come against it. That's why nature does not create a fully mature tree. A tree's growth period allows it to establish a foundation of roots to weather storms and give it stability to shelter other creatures and serve as a witness to God's presence.

We are much like those trees. We can find the strength to sustain ourselves against the forces in life that seek to topple us only in community. The living of life in real time and in the context of each other's lives gives us stability, meaning, identity, and love. These are the roots that form a solid system of interdependence with other members of the community. This is the model that has worked throughout history.

When we seek to live virtually, or apart from each other, none of these characteristics are ours to share. Or even to experience. Those who rely on social media as their community are relying on an environment that was not meant to provide such community and is incapable of the complex relationships a true community requires. Simply, the physical intertwining of our roots is impossible in a virtual context. So those who have substituted this artificial community for the real one and then expect to receive from it all the things they receive from a real community will awaken one day to find the emptiness of artificial satisfaction. As a result, we get confused as to what we can expect from our virtual world. We have believed the lie, and like all lies, it leads us into a dead end of human experience.

Unfortunately, people have not only begun living in this artificial community, but they have also built their homes on this foundation, expecting to find fulfillment that is unachievable. Ultimately, the more time people spend in an artificial community, the more likely they will topple when forces come against them. Often, their purpose in life will topple as well. And if we have no purpose, the next logical step in someone's mind could be that neither does anyone else. Daily, we see this mindset acted out in random acts of rage, suicide, or anger. These acts are often the response of the logical conclusion that comes to many, namely that they don't matter. And if they don't matter, they might even decide that other people don't matter either.

So if no one matters and there is no true community to be a part of to offset that way of thinking, then they can come to the conclusion that they can walk into a public place and randomly take lives. Society then looks for a *reason* for such random violence and can only point to mental illness or the availability of guns. The real answer is much deeper than that, but our politically correct culture refuses to address those issues because they do not fit into the box we've built to keep out the discussion about absolute truth or truth beyond ourselves. If there is no absolute truth to which we are accountable, you might reason that there's no absolute standard for right or wrong as well. In that case, a Bernie Madoff or anyone else can create intricate models of deception to rob people of their life savings and ruin their lives.

We have looked everywhere for possible answers to the way in which our society has seemingly imploded with rage, lack of civility, corruption, and open and outright disregard for others. Could it be that the absence of true community is the answer? This artificial online community has created such distortion of the inherent value of others that there is no longer any inhibition to protecting those values.

To the Christ-follower, though, there is an answer, and there is an objective reality to truth.

Jesus embodied true community. He still calls us today to follow his model for community, which is the sharing of life in common. The communists and the utopian socialists had it all wrong. It was never about sharing goods and services; it was always about sharing each other. Community started as the Trinity before creation and continues to this day. Notice that God used plural pronouns in Genesis 1:26: "Let *us* make mankind in *our* image, in *our* likeness" (NIV, emphasis added). He created the earth and humanity for a distinct purpose: to exhibit his glory and have fellowship with us. He has set in motion principles for the maximum efficiency and coexistence of his creation to ultimately reflect that community.

Knowing your purpose in life is the ultimate freedom. And it creates true communities where freedom can exist because it is others-directed. It exists for the common good *only* in communion with each other. There is no common good without a community. It's like love. It has no definition until one gives it away. It's not love if it is self-contained. I think you get the picture.

> Experience the joy of community
> that only comes through
> communion with others.

The internet community consists of voices telling us every day that we do not have a purpose other than to fulfill ourselves. If you feel that serving the greater good is about you, think again. It's never about you; it's beyond you. If it's only about you, then it is not true community. And if it's not true community, you'll never have the roots to sustain the tsunamis that will come against you. Like those redwood trees, it takes time to grow those roots so we can become the people we were meant to be. Give your roots time to grow deep and intermingle with others who will help you stand during difficult times. Experience the joy of community that only comes through communion with others.

America will become good again when we eliminate the virtual shortcuts to community in our lives.

The Secret Sauce That Makes It All Work

"Nothing is more wonderful than the art of being free, but nothing is harder to learn how to use than freedom." Alexis de Tocqueville wrote this in *Democracy in America*, and this quote of his hits on what I consider to be the necessary ingredient for making America good again: the combination of moral freedom grounded in a faith beyond us that establishes the benchmark and plumb line for that freedom. It is accountability beyond ourselves. And beyond government.

When the state or any other group seeks to control what we think and say and fosters a fear of expression, that is the beginning of totalitarianism. We see this dangerous movement happening on our college campuses in particular. What was the ground for free speech a generation ago has become a playground for the politically correct elite to suppress any view differing from their own. This mindset has carried over into our political discourse as well.

> When you remove the mystery
> from something unknown,
> fear and misunderstanding wane.

When we cower to those forces in our culture that tell us to rename our symbols because someone might be insulted, it creates division, not tolerance. The freedom to display our symbols and discuss our heritages provides a basis for understanding the greatness of our country. Hiding them encourages ignorance. And we all know what ignorance breeds: suspicion, racism, and hate.

I'll give you an example. When my daughter was perhaps five or six, we were driving by our town hall, which was decorated with a crèche, a menorah, and a Santa. Political correctness would prefer we remove the crèche and menorah. Fortunately, that did not happen in my town. Anyway, the crèche was familiar to my daughter as was Santa. But she asked me about the menorah. I then had the privilege of using that symbol as a teaching opportunity to explain the story of the miracle of how one day's worth of oil lasted for eight and how the Maccabees, with God's help, freed their people from their oppressors.

I took this opportunity to remove some of the mystery from what had been, up to that point, unknown to my daughter. You see, when you remove the mystery from something unknown, fear and misunderstanding wane. And that is the beginning of tolerance. Awareness and education mitigate intolerance. Political correctness encourages disinformation.

To truly make America good again, our pulpits, whether they be in a church, the street corner, or via your mobile platform, must once again be "aflame with righteousness."

ABOUT THE AUTHOR

Joe Battaglia is a broadcaster, author (*A New Suit for Lazarus, The Politically Incorrect Jesus, That's My Dad, Fathers Say,* and *Unfriended: Finding True Community in a Disconnected Culture*), and founder and president of Renaissance Communications, a media company whose mission is to provide media platforms for gifted communicators of biblical truth. His clients include Dr. Steve Brown and his nationally syndicated radio program *Key Life*, Prison Fellowship, Affirm Films/Sony Pictures Entertainment, Sight & Sound Entertainment, actress/director Shari Rigby, and author/Bible teacher Kim Crabill. Joe is also co-executive producer of the nationally syndicated radio program *Keep the Faith*, the #1 faith-based music radio program in the nation with a weekly audience of nearly two million.

For over seventeen years, Joe has also been involved in the promotion of highly successful hit movies to the faith-based marketplace, such as *The Passion of the Christ, The Lion, The Witch & The Wardrobe, The Polar Express, Facing the Giants, Fireproof, Courageous, Soul Surfer, Son of God, God's Not Dead, Heaven Is For Real, Miracles From Heaven, Risen, War Room, The Star, I Can Only Imagine*, and *I Still Believe*.

Highly active in the Christian music industry, Joe served on the board of Gospel Music Association (GMA) for nineteen years, was chairman of the National Christian Radio Association (NCRS) for fourteen years, and currently sits on the boards of the National Religious Broadcasters and WAY Media.

Prior to forming Renaissance in 1992, Joe was VP of Communicom Corp. of America, the parent company of WWDJ/New York, WZZD/Philadelphia, and KSLR/San Antonio. He was with Communicom for over eighteen years, eight as general manager of the flagship station WWDJ from 1982–1990. From 1979–1995, he also was a partner in Living Communications, parent company of WLIX, Long Island and WLVX, Hartford, CT.

He attended Boston University, graduating magna cum laude with a Bachelor of Science in journalism.

Joe lives in New Jersey and has one daughter.